HOW DOES A
TV WORK?

BY ISAAC ASIMOV AND ELIZABETH KAPLAN

Gareth Stevens Publishing
MILWAUKEE

For a free color catalog describing Gareth Stevens' list of high-quality books, call
1-800-542-2595 (USA) or 1-800-461-9120 (Canada). Gareth Stevens' Fax: (414) 225-0377.

Library of Congress Cataloging-in-Publication Data

Asimov, Isaac.
    How does a TV work? / by Isaac Asimov and Elizabeth Kaplan.
    p. cm. — (Ask Isaac Asimov)
    Includes bibliographical references and index.
    Summary: Provides a simple explanation of the technology involved in transmitting and receiving television signals.
    ISBN 0-8368-0804-5
    1. Television—Juvenile literature. [1. Television.] I. Kaplan, Elizabeth, 1956-. II. Title. III. Series: Asimov, Isaac.
Ask Isaac Asimov.
TK6550.7.A85   1993
621.388—dc20
                                               92-32550

Edited, designed, and produced by
Gareth Stevens Publishing
1555 North RiverCenter Drive, Suite 201
Milwaukee, Wisconsin   53212, USA

Text © 1993 by Nightfall, Inc. and Martin H. Greenberg
End matter © 1993 by Gareth Stevens, Inc.
Format © 1993 by Gareth Stevens, Inc.

The book designer would like to thank Pewaukee TV, Banner TV, and Tony Dietzler for their expertise.

Picture Credits
pp. 2-3, Paul Miller/Advertising Art Studios, 1992; pp. 4-5, © Michael Bluest/Picture Perfect USA; pp. 6-7, © John Coster-Mullen/Third Coast Stock Source; pp. 8-9, Paul Miller/Advertising Art Studios, 1992; pp. 10-11, Paul Miller/Advertising Art Studios, 1992; pp. 12-13, Paul Miller/Advertising Art Studios, 1992; pp. 14-15, © R. Buckland/Barnaby's Picture Library; pp. 16-17, Paul Miller/Advertising Art Studios, 1992; pp. 18-19, Paul Miller/Advertising Art Studios, 1992; pp. 20-21, © Melanie Friend/Hutchison Library; pp. 22-23, Rick Karpinski, 1992; p. 24, Rick Karpinski, 1992

Cover photograph, the news set at WITI-TV6, Milwaukee, Wisconsin. This station has won many awards for its news-gathering ability. The final product is broadcast from this studio. Photo © Dave Whitman/WITI-TV, Gillett Communications of Milwaukee, Inc.

Series editor: Valerie Weber
Editors: Barbara J. Behm and Patricia Lantier-Sampon
Series designer: Sabine Beaupré
Book designer: Kristi Ludwig
Picture researcher: Diane Laska

Printed in the United States of America

2 3 4 5 6 7 8 9 98 97 96 95 94

Contents

Words that appear in the glossary are printed in **boldface** type the first time they occur in the text.

Modern-Day Wonders

Pick up your telephone. You can have a conversation with someone halfway around the world. Plug in your computer, and you can play games, do your homework, or send messages to a friend. Press a few buttons on

4

a microwave oven. You can have a steaming hot dinner in seconds. These are only some of the many wonders of **technology**.

Of all the products of modern technology, television, or TV, is by far the most popular. How does a TV work? Let's find out.

Changing Sound and Light

The musicians walk out on stage. They pick up their instruments with a flourish and strike the opening chords. Colored lights flash to the beat. The audience cheers wildly.

TV cameras record the sound and motion of the live concert. They change sound and light into a type of invisible energy called **electromagnetic waves**. These waves form a pattern, a code of the sound and motion recorded by the TV camera.

7

Waves in the Air

Towers located near the concert send
electromagnetic waves through the air.
These waves travel at the speed of light. But
buildings, mountains, and the surface of the

Earth block electromagnetic waves. So the waves are relayed to and from tall towers called broadcasting towers. TV stations also beam electromagnetic waves up to **satellites**. Satellites can strengthen the waves and broadcast them all over the world.

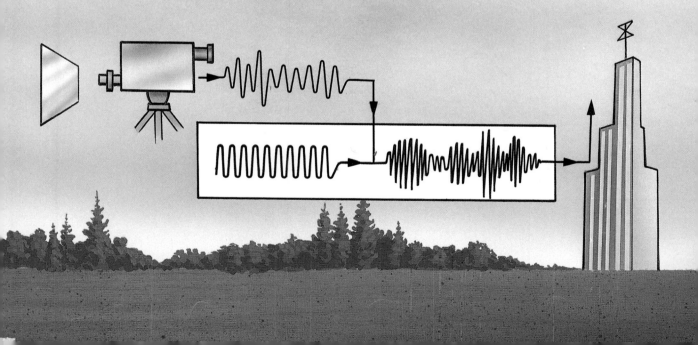

From the Air to Your TV

Although you can't feel them, electromagnetic waves are buzzing around you. The TV antenna picks up these waves.

The antenna is made of wires. Electro-magnetic waves push on **electrons**, tiny particles that flow through the wires. The electrons move in a pattern based on the motion of the electromagnetic waves. The antenna connects to other wires inside the TV. The TV changes the pattern of moving electrons into sound and pictures.

10

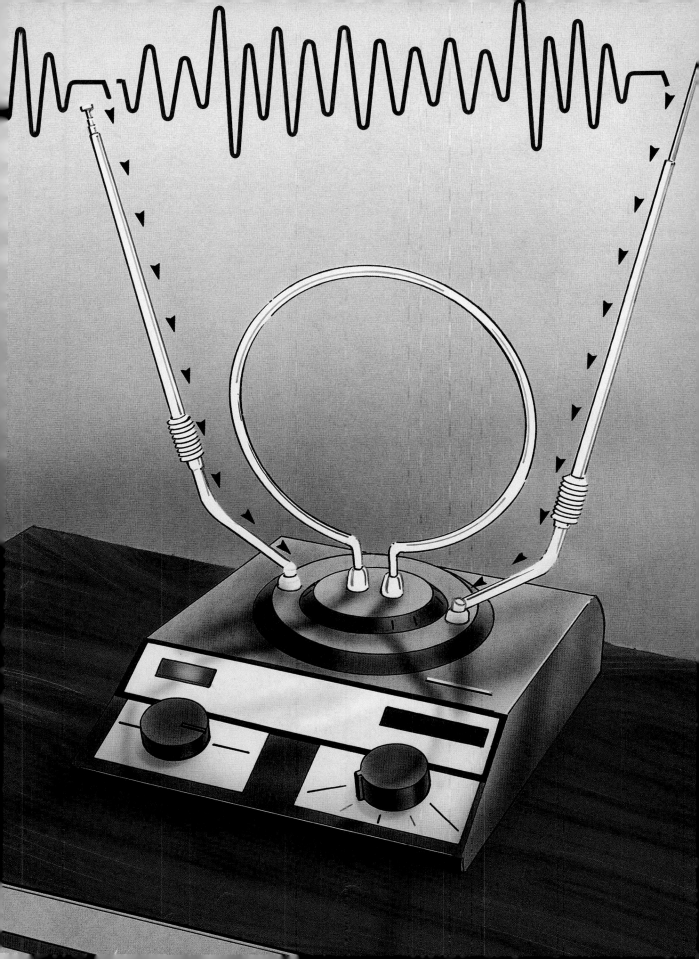

Sound from a Cone

A TV has a loudspeaker that changes patterns of moving electrons into sound. The loudspeaker has a magnet and a wire coil attached to a cone. The movement of electrons in the coil creates a **magnetic field**. When this field is strong, the coil is pushed and pulled forcefully by the magnet. This makes the cone **vibrate** with a loud sound. When the field is weak, the cone vibrates softly. These vibrations make the sounds that come from your TV.

Seeing Dots

One of TV's surprising secrets is that the
picture is not made up of solid lines and
shapes. It is made up of tiny dots. If you
look closely at the lit screen, you will see
these dots. Your eyes automatically blend
the dots together so you see solid shapes.

A TV camera records a scene as a pattern of
bright and dim dots. This dot pattern is
changed into the strong and weak electromagnetic waves that travel to your TV set.

14

Scanning the Picture

The electromagnetic waves enter a device in your TV called the scanner. The scanner shoots a beam of electrons at the back of the TV screen. When the beam hits the screen, the screen gives off a tiny dot of light. The stronger the electromagnetic wave, the stronger the electron beam. The stronger the electron beam, the brighter the dot of light. The beam moves rapidly back and forth behind the screen, creating the TV picture as a pattern of bright and dim dots.

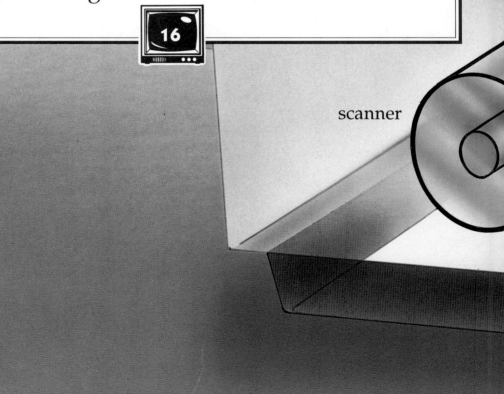

16

scanner

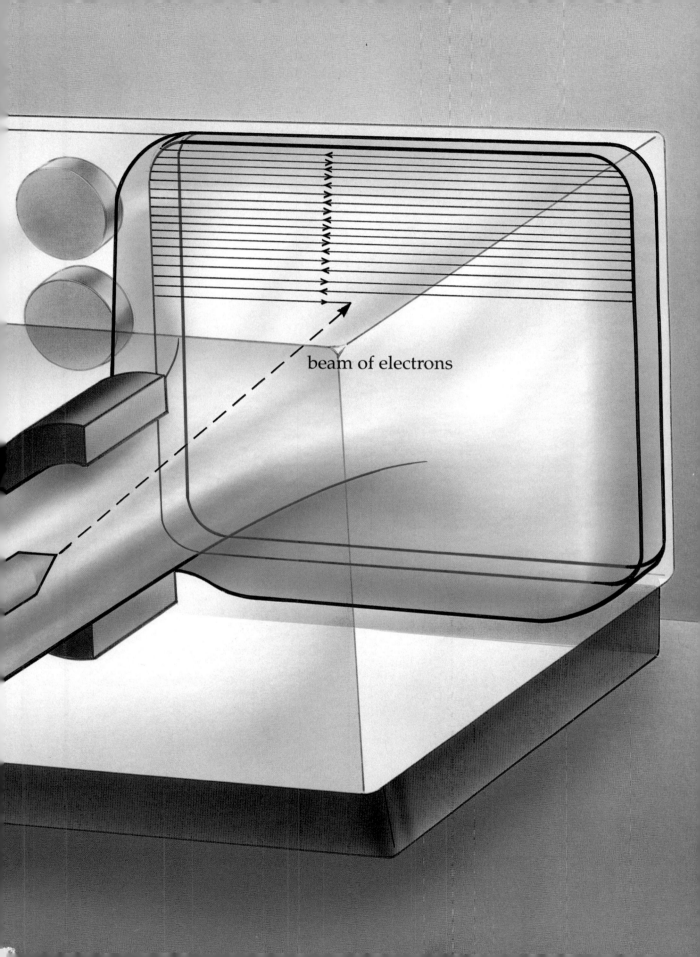

beam of electrons

Living Color

In a color TV, the scanner reads three separate signals to create the picture. One signal codes for red light. The second codes for green light. The third codes for blue light. The picture shows how these colors of light blend to create all the other colors. Note that if red, green, and blue light are all blended equally, white light results. With a color TV, each dot is made up of a different mixture of the three primary colors of light.

Cable Television

Watch a court trial in action; see a recent movie; shop for gifts. You can do all these things from your home if you have cable TV. With cable TV, signals travel down a thick

20

rope of wires or fibers called a cable. Your TV is connected to the cable and receives the signals. The signals are always sharp and clear. In the mountains and in cities with tall buildings, people sometimes use cable to get clear reception for all channels.

An Open Question

TV can be educational as well as entertaining. In the future, you might receive your education at home, watching your teachers on TV. Television technology will let you do all of your shopping, get library books, go to college, and get a job without leaving home. Will television make our lives better? What do you think?

22

More Books to Read

Let's Visit a Television Station by Carol Freed (Troll Associates)
Ramona: Behind the Scenes of a Television Show by Elaine Scott
   (Morrow Junior Books)
Television and Radio by Louis Sabin (Troll Associates)
TV and Video by N. S. Barrett (Franklin Watts)

Places to Write

Here are some places you can write for more information about
television and its history. Be sure to tell them exactly what you
want to know. Give them your full name and address so they can
write back to you.

National Museum
   Division of Electricity
   Smithsonian Institution
900 Jefferson Drive, SW
Room 2410
Washington, D.C. 20560

Museum of Television and
   Radio
25 West 52nd Street
New York, New York 10019

Museum of Broadcast
   Communications
800 South Wells Street
Chicago, Illinois 60607

Glossary

electromagnetic waves (ih-LEK-trow-mag-NET-ik waves): waves
   of energy that travel at the speed of light. Television signals,
   radio waves, and light are all types of electromagnetic waves.

electron (ee-LEHK-trahn): a tiny charged particle that forms part
   of the atom. The movement of electrons causes electricity.

23

magnetic field: the area of magnetic force that is produced around a magnet or is made by moving electrons.

satellite (SAT-uhl-ite): a spacecraft that circles the Earth. Satellites can receive television signals and transmit them to all parts of the globe.

technology (tehk-NAH-luh-jee): the use of scientific principles to produce things that are useful to people.

vibrate (VIE-brayte): to move back and forth rapidly.

Index